Coelenterates From Labrador And Newfoundland: Collected By Owen Bryant From July To October, 1908

Henry Bryant Bigelow

In the interest of creating a more extensive selection of rare historical book reprints, we have chosen to reproduce this title even though it may possibly have occasional imperfections such as missing and blurred pages, missing text, poor pictures, markings, dark backgrounds and other reproduction issues beyond our control. Because this work is culturally important, we have made it available as a part of our commitment to protecting, preserving and promoting the world's literature. Thank you for your understanding.

CŒLENTERATES FROM LABRADOR AND NEWFOUNDLAND, COLLECTED BY MR. OWEN BRYANT FROM JULY TO OCTOBER, 1908

BY

HENRY B. BIGELOW

Of the Museum of Comparative Zoology, Cambridge, Massachusetts

---

No. 1706.—From the Proceedings of the United States National Museum,
Vol. 37, pages 301-320, with Plates 30-32

Published December 14, 1909

Washington
Government Printing Office
1909

CŒLENTERATES FROM LABRADOR AND NEWFOUNDLAND, COLLECTED BY MR. OWEN BRYANT FROM JULY TO OCTOBER, 1908.

By Henry B. Bigelow,

Of the Museum of Comparative Zoology, Cambridge, Massachusetts.

The cœlenterates described in the following pages were collected by Mr. Owen Bryant at various points along the east coast of Labrador and the south and east coasts of Newfoundland during the summer of 1908. The collection consists of twelve species of Craspedotæ, one siphonophore, three Scyphomedusæ, and three ctenophores. None of the species are new, but inasmuch as the medusa fauna of this region has not previously been studied, the records are of importance from the standpoint of geographical distribution. As might have been expected from our knowledge of other groups of animals, several of the species were previously known only from Greenland and from northern Europe. Such are *Sarsia princeps* and *Ptychogastria polaris*. *Catablema vesicaria*, *Bougainvillea superciliaris*, *Staurophora laciniata*, and *Aglantha rosea* were already known from both sides of the north Atlantic, so that the occurrence of these forms in the region in question, bridging over the gap in their known distribution, was to be expected. The capture of *Æginopsis laurentii* is of especial interest, since there was already good reason to believe that this species would be found to be of general boreal occurrence when the Arctic coasts of North America were more thoroughly explored from the faunistic standpoint.

Although all the species are well known, two, *Catablema vesicaria* and *Æginopsis laurentii*, are of great systematic interest. Fortunately both are represented by such good series that, in the former, I have been able to make a study of the tentacles and of the gonads, and in the latter to verify many points of anatomy important in the general classification of the Narcomedusæ. It has been a pleasure to work on specimens of Medusæ so excellently preserved as those prepared by Mr. Bryant.

LIST OF SPECIES.

CRASPEDOTÆ.

	Page
Sarsia mirabilis L. Agassiz	302
Sarsia princeps (Haeckel)	303
Tiara pileata (Forskàl)	303
Catablema vesicaria (A. Agassiz)	304
Bougainvillea superciliaris (L. Agassiz)	305
Lizzia octopunctata (Sars)	306
Staurophora laciniata L. Agassiz	307
Milicertum campanula (Fabricius)	308
Obelia geniculata (Linnæus)	310
Ptychogastria polaris Allman	310
Aglantha rosea (Forbes)	312
Æginopsis laurentii Brandt	314

SIPHONOPHORÆ.

Diphyopsis campanulifera (Eschscholtz)	316

SCYPHOMEDUSÆ.

Haliclystus auricula H. J. Clark	316
Aurelia flavidula Péron and Lesueur	316
Cyanea arctica Péron and Lesueur	316

CTENOPHORÆ.

Pleurobrachia pileus (Fabricius)	316
Mertensia ovum (Fabricius)	316
Beroe cucumis Fabricius	317

DESCRIPTION OF SPECIES.

CRASPEDOTÆ.

ANTHOMEDUSÆ.

SARSIA MIRABILIS L. Agassiz.

Plate 30, fig. 2.

Sarsia mirabilis L. AGASSIZ, '49, p. 228, pls. 4, 5.

One specimen, about 10 mm. high, from St. Pierre, off Newfoundland, October 1, probably belongs to this well-known species, judging from its size and from the color of its tentacular bulbs and ocelli. Unfortunately, however, both manubrium and tentacles are so strongly contracted as to make positive identification impossible.

S. mirabilis is known not only from the Atlantic coast of North America, Baffin's Bay, Greenland, and probably northern Europe (Hartlaub, :07, p. 39), but also from the Pacific coast of North America, a fact omitted in my summary of the Pacific *Sarsiæ* (:09). It is likewise recorded, though with reservation as to its true identity, from the coast of Chile, by Hartlaub (:07, p. 39).

SARSIA PRINCEPS (Haeckel).

Plate 30, fig. 1.

Codonium princeps HAECKEL, '79, p. 13, pl. 1, fig. 3.

For the synonymy of this species, see Hartlaub, :07, p. 47.

One specimen, 14 mm. high, St. Pierre, off Newfoundland, October 1. I entirely agree with Browne (:03) and Hartlaub (:07) that this species is a typical *Sarsia*, and that the genus *Codonium* of Haeckel ('79) is a synonym of *Sarsia*. For the history of the species, see Hartlaub, :07, p. 47.

The single individual (pl. 30, fig. 1) is readily identified with *S. princeps* on account of its close resemblance to Hartlaub's figure. This species is one of the best defined in the difficult genus *Sarsia*, being distinguishable by its large size, the pronounced apical projection of the gelatinous bell, the presence of a "stiel-canal," and especially by the jagged outlines of the radial canals. The latter are visible in the photograph (pl. 30, fig. 1); they seem, however, to have been overlooked by both Browne (:03) and Grönberg ('98), although recently mentioned and figured by Hartlaub (:07). In the single specimen both manubrium and tentacles are contracted, but in the former the distal gastric portion is sharply defined from the more proximal region which bears the sexual products.

Color.—Manubrium and tentacles, after preservation with formalin, are reddish, the minute ocelli black.

This species, known from various localities on the Arctic coasts of Europe, from Barents Sea, and from Spitzbergen, has also been recorded by Vanhöffen ('97) from the west coast of Greenland, so that its occurrence in Labrador and Newfoundland was to be expected.

TIARA PILEATA (Forskål).

Plate 30, fig. 5; plate 31, fig. 7.

Medusa pileata FORSKÅL, 1775, p. 110; 1776, pl. 33, fig. D.
Tiara pileata L. AGASSIZ, '62, p. 347.

This species is represented in the collection by nine specimens, taken 30 miles southeast of Nain, Labrador, August 18, ranging in diameter from 6–15 mm. The largest specimen is apparently sexually mature and has 37 tentacles. Differences in the shape of the basal bulbs of the tentacles offer a ready distinction between this species and *Catablema vesicaria*, and are of much assistance in instances where both margin and gonads are damaged (compare pl. 30, fig. 5, with pl. 31, fig. 7). *Tiara pileata* is one of the most widely distributed of Atlantic Hydromedusæ. On the coast of Europe it is common from Norway to the Mediterranean (Haeckel, '79; Browne, :03) and in American waters it has been recorded from Maine to Rhode Island (Fewkes, *Turris episcopalis*).

CATABLEMA VESICARIA (A. Agassiz).

Plate 30, figs. 3, 4; plate 31, fig. 6.

Turris vesicaria A. AGASSIZ, '62a, p. 97.
Catablema vesicaria HAECKEL, '79, p. 64.

This interesting boreal species is represented in the collection by 27 specimens in various stages of development. The adult has been so well described and figured by A. Agassiz ('65), by Haeckel ('79 "*C. campanula*") and by Maas (:04) that no extended account is necessary here. However, young stages have not previously been described, so far as I am aware.

In general form the series agrees closely with the figures of A. Agassiz and of Maas, an extreme development of the apical gelatinous projection (pl. 30, figs. 3, 4) being an important characteristic of the species.

Tentacles.—The largest specimen (19 mm. high by 17 mm. in diameter), which is in about the stage figured by A. Agassiz ('65, fig. 262), has twenty-two well-developed tentacles and twenty rudimentary tentacular knobs rather irregularly distributed. In another specimen of nearly as great size (18 by 14.5 mm.) the development of the tentacles has progressed somewhat further, there being thirty-seven large and only two rudimentary tentacles. According to Haeckel from thirty-six to forty-eight tentacles are finally formed. The smallest specimen, 3 mm. high by 3 mm. in diameter, has four large radial tentacles, four somewhat smaller interradial tentacles, and eight minute adradial tentacular knobs. This condition indicates that the order of development of tentacles is successively radial, interradial, adradial. In normal development subradial rudiments next appear. But in all the present specimens the development of additional tentacles, after the first three series, is irregular, no two quadrants of any specimen being precisely alike. Thus in an individual 10 mm. high by 9 mm. in diameter, in which the first traces of gonads are visible, inter- and adradial tentacles have alone appeared in one quadrant, while in all the other quadrants subradial rudiments are also present. In still later stages the development of additional tentacles is so irregular that the normal succession is entirely masked.

The tentacular bases are laterally compressed and bear spurs clasping the exumbrella (pl. 31, fig. 6, *T. Ra.*). It is not unlikely that their outline, which appears constant, will prove to be of specific significance. Ocelli are recorded for this species by A. Agassiz ('65), and can be determined on a few specimens in the present series. In most cases, however, none are distinguishable. In all probability they have disappeared as the result of preservation, since neither Haeckel ('79) nor Maas (:04) observed any such organs in the preserved specimens which they examined.

Gonads.—The most important character which distinguishes *Catablema* from the related genera *Pandea*, *Tiara*, and *Clavula*,[a] is the form of the gonads. In *C. vesicaria* these organs have been well figured both by A. Agassiz and by Maas, and the latter author has pointed out the importance of the gonads in the classification of the Tiaridæ. The sexual organs, as in all Tiaridæ, are purely interradial (though in adults this position is largely masked by their growth); and each gonad is primarily a horseshoe-shaped structure. The feature in which *Catablema* differs from related genera is that the interradial portion of each gonad (connecting the two arms of the horseshoe) consists of a series of distinct vertical folds (pl. 30, fig. 3, *go*).

Maas has considered an extreme development of lateral diverticulæ on the radial and circular canals as characteristic of *Catablema*. In this respect, however, the genus is so closely approached by *Clavula* that it is impossible to draw any line between the two. In the larger specimens in the present series the diverticulæ on the radial canals are well developed, some simple and some branched (pl. 31, fig. 6). On the circular canal, however, they are much less prominent, forming merely a jagged outline. This is a general condition no more complex than I have described and figured for the Pacific *Clavula fontata* (Bigelow, :09).

Color.—After preservation with formalin, stomach, canals, and tentacles are pale orange, and the gonads a deeper shade of the same color.

Catablema vesicaria is a purely boreal species. On the American coast it has once been recorded from Massachusetts Bay, and never from south of Cape Cod. It is common along the Labrador coast. Haeckel ('79) records it from Greenland, and Maas (:04) from the Arctic Ocean near Bear Island.

BOUGAINVILLEA SUPERCILIARIS (L. Agassiz).

Plate 31, fig. 2.

Hippocrene superciliaris L. AGASSIZ, '49, p. 273, pls. 1-3.
Bougainvillea superciliaris L. AGASSIZ, '62, pp. 289, 344, pl. 27, figs. 1-7.

Labrador, 30 miles southeast of Nain, surface; 5 specimens, all about 6.5 mm. high by 5 to 5.5 mm. in diameter.

I can add little to the excellent accounts and figures of this species which we owe to L. Agassiz ('49) and to Hartlaub ('97).

The specimens, though larger than any observed by L. Agassiz, are slightly smaller than the largest seen by Hartlaub, who records individuals 8 mm. in height. Haeckel ('79) has recorded specimens 12 mm. in height, but Hartlaub questions whether these, in view of

---

[a] For the medusan genus commonly known, since Lesson, as *Turris*, the name *Clavula*, applied by Strethill Wright (Proc. Edinburgh Phys. Soc., vol. 2, 1859) to the hydroid stage of *Turris neglecta* Lesson, must be used since the name "*Turris*" is preoccupied by Bolton for a genus of mollusca.

their large size and small number (10-15) of tentacles in each bundle, do not belong to a distinct variety.

The greatest number of tentacles in any bundle of the present series is fourteen; Agassiz figures 11-14, and Hartlaub has counted as many as twenty-two in larger individuals from Heligoland.

The oral tentacles agree in their branching with L. Agassiz' figures. In most cases they branch dichotomously four times, occasionally, however, five times. But this is not their final condition, since Hartlaub has observed instances in which branching took place six and seven times.

In the short squarish outline of the manubrium and in the fact that this organ is situated on a short peduncle (pl. 31, fig. 2), as well as in the thickness of the gelatinous substance of the bell, and in the broadness of the radial canals, the specimens agree closely with the accounts and figures of previous students.

The color is that recorded by Hartlaub, the entoderm of the manubrium being reddish brown, the tentacular bulbs brownish red, the ocelli black.

B. superciliaris is a species of wide distribution. On the Atlantic coast of America it is known to occur as far south as Woods Hole, Massachusetts, and it is a common species thence northward to Labrador, and perhaps to Greenland (Haeckel), and, as already noted, it is known from Heligoland (Hartlaub).

LIZZIA OCTOPUNCTATA (Sars).

Plate 31, figs. 3-5.

Cytæis octopunctata Sars, '35, p. 28, pl. 6, fig. 14.
Lizzia octopunctata Forbes, '48, p. 64; pl. 12, fig. 13.

The generic distinctions between the Bougainvilleidæ with eight tentacle groups have been well drawn by Maas (:05), who recognizes two genera, *Lizzia* and *Rathkea*, separated by the structure of the labial arms, as well as by the number of marginal tentacles in each group. The various other genera founded by Haeckel, namely, *Lizusa*, *Lizzella*, and *Margellium* were, as shown by Vanhöffen ('89), founded upon young stages.

Thanks to the studies of A. Agassiz ('65, "*Lizzia grata*") and Browne ('96, "*Margellium octopunctatum*") the stages in growth of *L. octopunctata* from the liberation of the medusa-bud to the adult, are now well known, and to the latter author I refer the reader for its complex synonymy ('96, p. 477).

The collection contains a series of about 200 specimens of this species from Fogo Island, Newfoundland, July 28, including both budding and sexual phases, as well as numerous young stages.

Sexual and budding phases are of about the same size, the largest specimens of each being about 4 mm. high by 3.5 mm. in diameter.

In most of the specimens the oral appendages are in the condition shown in the photograph (pl. 31, fig. 5), there being four sessile nematocyst knobs at each corner of the mouth. Earlier stages, such as are figured by A. Agassiz ('65, fig. 257) are to be seen in smaller specimens. In the adult condition, according to A. Agassiz, there are seven nematocyst organs in each cluster and the same condition is recorded by Browne ('96). This type of oral appendage, as has been pointed out by Maas (:05) is entirely different from the branched oral tentacles of *Rathkea*, and forms sufficient grounds for separating the two genera.

The numbers recorded by A. Agassiz and by Browne for the groups of tentacles, five for each radial, three for each interradial group, appear to be the final ones. At least, I have never seen them surpassed.

In the earliest stage in the development of tentacles which I have observed, the bud being still attached to the manubrium of the parent, there is one tentacle in each group, radial or interradial, the radials being much the largest.

Young medusæ, at liberation, have three tentacles in each radial group, the central one being much the largest, and one in each interradial group. The adult number of tentacles is usually attained, as described by A. Agassiz ('65), by the development of an additional pair of lateral tentacles in each group, radial or interradial, but the formation of additional tentacles is rather irregular, as Browne has observed.

Color.—In the preserved specimens the manubrium in the budding phase is very pale reddish, in the sexual phase its entoderm is of a much deeper reddish brown tint. In both phases the tentacular bulbs are of a deep chocolate brown. These structures are recorded by Hargitt (:05) as being "pinkish, tending to brown, and even blackish in rare cases."

This species was previously known to occur commonly in Massachusetts Bay and south of Cape Cod in the Woods Hole region and at Newport, Rhode Island. It is not known from south of Long Island Sound. In European waters it is known from Norway south to the coast of France.

LEPTOMEDUSÆ.

STAUROPHORA LACINIATA L. Agassiz.

Staurophora laciniata L. AGASSIZ, '49, p. 308, pl. 7.

One specimen, 70 mm. in diameter; Fogo Island, Newfoundland, July 28; surface.

The single specimen, which has well-developed gonads, is of only medium size, since this species frequently attains a diameter of 150 mm.

Staurophora laciniata is a common boreal species. On the American coast it occurs only occasionally south of Cape Cod. Hartlaub ('97) has recorded what is probably the young of this species from Heligoland, and it is probable that the *S. arctica* of Haeckel ('79) from Spitzbergen is identical with *S. laciniata*.

MELICERTUM CAMPANULA (Fabricius).

Plate 31, fig. 1; plate 32, fig. 1.

Medusa campanula FABRICIUS, 1780, No. 360.
Melicertum campanula A. AGASSIZ, '62a, p. 96; '65, p. 130, figs. 202–214.

Haeckel ('79) has pointed out that the identity of Fabricius' specimens with those subsequently described by A. Agassiz ('65) under the name *Melicertum campanula* is doubtful, owing to the unsatisfactory nature of Fabricius' account. But since it is improbable that any better identification of Fabricius' material can ever be made, it will add to the stability of nomenclature to accept the identification of A. Agassiz, who has fully described and figured the species.

This common northern form is represented in the collection as follows:

Fogo Island, Newfoundland, July 19, nine specimens in early growth.

St. Pierre, off Newfoundland, three specimens, all about 15 mm. high by 12 mm. in diameter, with mature sexual products.

Although this species has been thoroughly figured and described by A. Agassiz ('65), the structure of the tentacular organs deserves fresh study, since Maas (:05) has raised the question whether or not there are cirri and knobs as well as developed tentacles. Haeckel ('79) has made the presence or absence of such secondary marginal organs the basis for generic distinction, *Melicertidium* having, *Melicertum* lacking them. Maas ('97, :05), however, has abandoned this criterion, and suggests, from A. Agassiz' figures, that on fresh examination, cirri and knobs will be found in *M. campanula*. The evidence in the present series indicates, however, that there is only one class of marginal organ in this species, *i. e.*, tentacles, though these develop continuously and it is probable that not all ever reach the final condition.

In the earliest stage in the present series (specimen 1.75 mm. high by 2 mm. in diameter), there are eight large radial tentacles, eight well-developed, though smaller, interradial tentacles, and in each octant two adradial elements which show all stages from mere knobs to very small tentacles with basal bulbs and terminal filaments. Several of the smallest elements, moreover, closely resemble the cirrus-like structures figured by A. Agassiz.

At a slightly later stage the adradials in seven octants have attained their definitive tentacular form, though they are still smaller than the interradials. In the eighth octant, however, one of the radials is still a mere knob. In seven octants a fourth series of marginal structures, subradials, ranging from minute knobs to fully formed, though small, tentacles, has likewise appeared. In the eighth octant, however, no subradials are yet present.

From this stage onward new members of the tentacular series are formed in irregular succession. In an individual 5.5 mm. in diameter by 6 mm. high there are, besides the radials, thirty-six tentacles, respectively 5, 4, 4, 4, 4, 6, 4, 5, to the octant, and these show all stages in development. In a slightly larger individual (6.5 mm. in diameter by 6 mm. high) the six subradials in one octant have all attained tentacular form, although in other octants both knobs and cirri are present.

In the most advanced specimen (15 mm. high by 12 mm. in diameter) there is a total of 129 tentacular structures, of which 72 have attained full tentacular form, the remainder showing early stages in growth. In one octant of this specimen (pl. 31, fig. 1) there are, between the two radial canals, nine large tentacles (T^1), four small tentacles (T^2), cirri (ci), and knobs.

This series shows that there is no morphologic distinction in this species, between the various marginal structures, knobs and cirri being merely early stages, partly perhaps contraction phases, in the growth of tentacles. But, inasmuch as even in mature specimens many such early stages are present, and since additional members of the tentacular series are formed continuously, I doubt whether a stage is ever reached in which only fully developed tentacles are present. However, although we can draw no sound distinction between knobs and cirri on the one hand and tentacles on the other, I agree with Maas that the distinction between the two genera *Melicertum* and *Melicertidium* is invalid, though on a different ground, namely, that the knobs and cirri in *Melicertidium* and in *Melicertum proboscifera* (Maas '97) are probably nothing more than early stages in the growth of tentacles, just as they are in *M. campanula*.

M. campanula is an abundant species in American waters from Labrador to Cape Cod, and it is known to occur as far south as Woods Hole, Massachusetts. A closely allied form, *M. octocostata* Sars, is known along the European coast from Norway to England. The latter was made by Haeckel ('79), the type of his genus *Melicertidium*, but from the brief account of Browne ('95) it is evident that the "knobs" are nothing more than young tentacles. It is not improbable that *M. octocostata* may finally prove identical with *M. campanula*, but until it is better known it is wisest to retain both species.

OBELIA GENICULATA (Linnæus).

Sertularia geniculata LINNÆUS, 1776, No. 1312.
Obelia geniculata ALLMAN, '64, p. 372.

The collection contains many specimens of *Obelia* from St. Pierre, off Newfoundland, October, and from Fogo Island, Newfoundland, July 28.

They are all far advanced in development. In the position of the gonads they resemble the figures of *O. geniculata* given by Böhm ('78, pl. 3, figs. 1-34). This species has already been recorded by Nutting ('99) from Woods Hole, Massachusetts, and on the coast of Europe is widely distributed. The identification can, however, be only provisional, inasmuch as a knowledge of the hydroid stages is essential for final determination.

TRACHOMEDUSÆ.

The collection contains two species of Trachomedusæ, one belonging to the remarkable and still obscure genus *Ptychogastria*, the other to *Aglantha*.

PTYCHOGASTRIA POLARIS Allman.

Ptychogastria polaris ALLMAN, '78, p. 290, figs. 1-3.

Four specimens, 13 to 21 mm. in diameter, from between Cape Mugford and Hebron, Labrador, August 23, in the dredge, from 60 fathoms. Unfortunately, all of the specimens are in such poor condition that I can do little more than corroborate the excellent account of this species which we owe to Browne (:03), who has shown that the description by Haeckel ('79, '81, *Pectyllis arctica*) is incorrect in several particulars. Its synonymy and history have recently been discussed by Maas (:06, p. 582). The most remarkable feature of *Ptychogastria* is the fact (demonstrated by Browne) that although the presence of free club-like otocysts undoubtedly places it among the Trachomedusæ, the gonads are situated not on the radial canals, but on folds of the walls of the manubrium. Maas, it is true, has doubted whether the sexual organs are truly stomachic. But my examination of the present specimens, in which the manubria were fairly well preserved, has convinced me that Browne is correct in maintaining that the gonads belong exclusively to the walls of the stomach and that no sexual products are developed on the radial canals.

The question whether or not there are sixteen distinct gonads, as Browne maintains, or whether Maas (:06, p. 483) is correct in saying that there are only eight, but that "Jede der 8 Gonaden erscheint übrigens durch die Ansatzlinie der Mesenteriums scharf zweigeteilt so dass man eigentlich von 16 Gonadenlamellen sprechen könnte" is one that can be answered only after a study of the development of these organs. It is certain, however, that in the adult the sexual organs are entirely discontinuous along the narrow line of attachment of the mesenteries to the manubrium, as well as in the interradii. In other words, in the adult the sixteen sexual masses are adradial. They may, however, be formed by the fission of eight primary gonads. Maas, in discussing the probable relationship of this genus, especially to *Crossota*, has suggested that possibly the eight radial ridges of the manubrium which bear the gonads are in reality basal dilations of the radial canals, so that "die 8 Aussackungen die die Gonaden versorgen, dem Boden der Radiärkanäle entsprechen, auch wenn letztere selbst, wie die Schnittbilder Browne's lehren, davon ganz anabhängig verlaufen" (:06, p. 483). But the conditions in the adult seem to me to lend no actual support to such a view, although a study of the development of the species may give a different result.

No sense organs were to be found in the present specimens. Browne, however, observed them, and found that their number was probably sixteen.

Tentacles.—I can add nothing to Browne's account except to note that in one specimen there is a single very large filiform tentacle about twice as long as the bell is high, arising from the tentacular scar between two of the tentacle groups. Allman, in the original account of the species, figured these large tentacles, but in Browne's specimens they were all broken off.

Ptychogastria polaris is certainly not an abyssal form, since all recent records of its capture are from comparatively shoal water. It has never, however, been taken on the surface, so far as I know. Judging from the presence of sucking pads on certain of its tentacles, Browne is probably correct in suggesting that it attaches itself to the bottom, as its near relative, *Pectanthis asteroides*, was seen to do by Haeckel ('81). However, as Browne has pointed out, the high degree of muscular development suggests that the species may be an active swimmer.

It is not worth while to speculate on the affinities of this remarkable genus until the young stages have been worked out, for only in that way can the nature of gonads and mesenteries be determined. In the meantime we may well follow Vanhöffen (:02) and Maas (:06) in associating it with *Crossota*, to which it is related by the arrangement of the several rows of tentacles.

Genus AGLANTHA.

Recent researches on this difficult genus have led most students to agree that in the North Atlantic two species are recognizable, *A. digitale*, with only four otocysts, of large size, and of Arctic distribution, and *A. rosea*, with eight otocysts, of much smaller size and of somewhat more southerly occurrence. Up to the present time the greatest size attained by *A. rosea* was supposed to be about 12 mm., whereas *A. digitale*, which has three or four well-marked geographical races, is known to grow to at least twice that height. Both species are known from both sides of the North Atlantic, but *A. rosea* has been recorded from the coast of America only once (Hargitt :05, *A. conica*, Woods Hole, Massachusetts). Inasmuch as *A. digitale* has been recorded from Massachusetts Bay and northward I expected the series in the present collection to belong to that species. But to my surprise all the specimens examined have eight otocysts, one in each octant, and must therefore be referred to *A. rosea*.

AGLANTHA ROSEA (Forbes).

Circe rosea FORBES, '48, p. 34, pl. 1, fig. 2.
Aglantha rosea BROWNE, '97, p. 833.

For the synonymy and history of this species, see Maas (:06).

Between Cape Sable and Cape Race, July 19, about 700 specimens, 1.5–8 mm. high; St. Pierre, off Newfoundland, October 1, about 100 specimens, 2–10 mm. high; Fogo Island, off Newfoundland, July 29, about 275 specimens, 2–7 mm. high; Gready Harbor, Labrador, 13 specimens, 13–25 mm. high; Cape Harrison, Labrador, August 13, 1 specimen, 21 mm. high; 30 miles southeast of Nain, Labrador, August 15, 129 specimens, 8.5–29 mm. high.

The series is extremely interesting, since it suggests that with regard to size and number of tentacles *Aglantha rosea* falls into two distinct races. The smaller of these agrees with *A. rosea*, as described by Browne (:03) and by Maas (:06). In this form gonads are first visible in specimens 2–3 mm. high, and are well developed in individuals 6–8 mm. high with 75–80 tentacles. The second race, in dimensions and number of tentacles, closely resembles *A. digitale*, var. *occidentalis* Maas, from which it can be distinguished only by the number of otocysts. Fortunately the present specimens were so well preserved that I was able to count these organs in many of the large individuals; otherwise I would no doubt have recorded them under the latter name. In this race, as is shown in the table, gonads first appear in specimens 7–10 mm. high, and they are well developed in specimens 14 mm. or more high. The largest individual in the series is 29 mm. high, a size previously thought to be attained, in this genus, only by *A. digitale*. In this specimen there are 214 tentacles. Such individuals, except for the number of otocysts, are indistinguishable from *A. digitale* as described by A. Agassiz ('65).

Measurements of specimens.

Locality.	Diameter.	Height.	Tentacles.	Otocysts.	Gonads.
	mm.	mm.			
Between Cape Sable and Cape Race, Newfoundland	1.5	2.0	23	4	None.
Do	2.0	3.5	34	6	Do.
Do	3.0	5.0	57	8	Very minute.
Fogo Island, Newfoundland	3.5	5.5	62	8	2 mm. long, male.
Do	4.0	7.0	71	7+	2 mm. long; large eggs.
Between Cape Sable and Cape Race, Newfoundland	4.5	7.0	73	8	Very small; sex?
Woods Hole, Massachusetts	5.0	14.0	108	7+	2 mm. long, male.
30 miles southeast of Nain, Labrador	6.0	10.0	115	8	Very minute.
Do	7.5	14.5	131	7+	Large female.
Do	8.0	22.0	163	8	Do.
Do	9.5	20.0	184	8	Do.
Gready Harbor, Labrador	11.0	22.5	167	8	Large male.
Do	13.0	23.0	173	8	Large female.
30 miles southeast of Nain, Labrador	13.0	29.0	214	6+	Large male.

The localities of capture suggest that the occurrence of these two races may indicate a geographic separation, inasmuch as all the specimens (between 1,000 and 1,100) from the south and east coasts of Newfoundland belong to the smaller, while all the specimens from north of the straits of Belle Isle belong to the larger race. But this distinction may prove to be of less significance than now appears, since it is impossible to distinguish the youngest stages of the two races, and since among the southern specimens several are apparently the young of the larger race. So far as the present collection goes there is no evidence that the difference between the two races is a seasonal one, because the smaller was taken in October as well as in July. I may further point out that should the difference between the two prove to be a case of geographic variation the distribution of the two, as illustrated by this collection, would indicate an entirely unexpected division, because the oceanographic conditions on the south coast of Newfoundland, where the effect of the Gulf Stream is often felt, differ markedly from those on the east coast, whereas there is no surface temperature change of importance between the east coast of Newfoundland and that of Labrador.

To settle definitely the question as to the relationship of the two races requires a more complete knowledge of their distribution than we now possess, and particularly a fresh study of their occurrence off the New England coast. In the meantime it is best not to burden the nomenclature of the genus with a fresh varietal name which may soon be found to be unwarranted.

NARCOMEDUSÆ.

The collection contains only one species of this order, *Æginopsis laurentii* Brandt.

ÆGINOPSIS LAURENTII Brandt.

Plate 32, figs. 2-6.

Æginopsis laurentii BRANDT, '38, p. 363, pl. 6.

Fogo Island, Newfoundland, July 28, 43 specimens, 1.5-7 mm. in diameter; Gready Harbor, Labrador, 1 specimen, 6 mm. in diameter; 30 miles southeast of Nain, Labrador, 1 specimen, 4 mm. and 1 specimen 13 mm. in diameter, the latter with well-developed gonads.

Though often recorded, certain anatomical features of this species are still imperfectly known. Especially is it desirable to determine whether or not a canal system is present, inasmuch as this point has never been examined in serial sections, although Maas (:06) has noted that surface views give no indication of the presence of either ring or peronial canals.

In general appearance the older specimens (pl. 3, fig. 2) closely resemble the figures given by Brandt ('38, pl. 6), the bell being of moderate height, and the tentacles arising fron the exumbral surface at a very high level.

Tentacles.—The most important feature of this genus is the fact that while there are only four tentacles, there are eight peroniæ, a fact clearly shown in Brandt's figures and accepted by all later authors.

Gastrovascular system.—The condition of the gastric pockets has been figured by Brandt ('38) and described by Maas (:06) (pl. 32, figs. 2, 3).

The series shows strong evidence that the sixteen gastric pockets of the adult are derived by subdivision from eight primary perradial pockets, one opposite each peronia. In the youngest specimen in the series, 2 mm. in diameter (pl. 32, fig. 4), the condition is as follows: opposite each of the four tentacles the primary pockets are bifid, but opposite the four peroniæ without tentacles the pockets are undivided, exactly as they are in the Cunanthidæ. At a slightly later stage (specimen 3 mm. in diameter) these latter pockets have become subdivided by shallow radial notches at their outer margins. Finally as growth proceeds a condition is reached (pl. 32, fig. 2) in which all eight primary gastric pockets are bifid to the same degree. Judging from these two stages it is reasonable to assume that there are originally four pockets opposite the tentacles, only that in their case the bifid condition is attained earlier than in the four pockets opposite the peroniæ without tentacles.

That the pockets are primarily radial in all the genera now grouped by Maas and by myself (:09) as Æginidæ is a generalization already proposed by Maas on theoretic grounds. But while it is no doubt true for *Æginopsis*, in view of the condition in *Ægina alternans* Bigelow (:09) in which there are only four interradial pockets, the question whether it holds for the entire family must remain open for the present.

A study of serial sections of the marginal region shows that there is no peripheral canal system in this genus. This fact strengthens the view upheld by Maas (:09) and by myself (:09) that the presence or absence of canals is of little value in classification, for while *Æginopsis* and *Solmundella* lack them entirely, *Ægina*, to which they are closely allied by the conformation both of the gastric pockets and of the sense organs, has this system well developed (Maas :05; Vanhöffen :08). This conclusion is opposed to the views of Vanhöffen (:08), who makes the presence or absence of canals a feature of prime importance in classification.

The structure of the sense organs is of interest, since they have not been described previously in this genus. The otocysts are of the ordinary æginid type (pl. 32, fig. 6), containing from 1 to 3 large otoliths and situated on prominent pads of the marginal ring, without otoporpæ. Since the latter organs do not occur, so far as known, in any of the Æginidæ, their absence is to be regarded as an important character. In the smallest individual there are sixteen otocysts, two in each octant. In older specimens octants were observed with three and with four otocysts, the latter number being the largest counted. The greatest number of otocysts in any one individual was twenty-six, in a specimen 7 mm. in diameter. Curiously enough in the largest specimen, 13 mm. in diameter, with mature gonads, there are only sixteen otocysts, two in each octant.

Gonads.—In the mature specimen, the only individual in which gonads are present, the sexual products, variously and irregularly lobed, occupy most of the surface of the gastric pockets (pl. 32, fig. 5). In the quadrant figured they overlap so much as to obscure in aboral views the septa separating the pockets, particularly in the case of the one in the radius of the peronia between the two tentacles.

The occurrence of this species on the coasts of Labrador and Newfoundland was to be expected since it is no doubt of general boreal distribution. It has previously been recorded from various localities off the north coast of Europe and from Greenland, as well as from Bering Strait (Brandt). It is probable also that the record of *Æ. mertensii* (Haeckel '79) from Japan belongs to this species.

SIPHONOPHORÆ.

DIPHYOPSIS CAMPANULIFERA (Eschscholtz).

Diphyes campanulifera ESCHSCHOLTZ, '29, p. 137.
Diphyopsis campanulifera CHUN, '88, p. 1159.

A single characteristic anterior nectophore of this species was taken on the surface at Fogo Island, Newfoundland, July 28. The record of this typical warm-water form is of interest as indicating the northward extent of the warm waters of the Gulf Stream.

SCYPHOMEDUSÆ.

HALICLYSTUS AURICULA H. J. Clark.

Haliclystus auricula H. J. CLARK, '63, p. 559.

Six specimens, St. Pierre, off Newfoundland, October 1; 5 fathoms. There are also specimens of this species in the Museum of Comparative Zoölogy, Cambridge, Massachusetts, from Indian Harbor, Labrador.

AURELIA FLAVIDULA Péron and Lesueur.

Aurelia flavidula PÉRON and LESUEUR, '09, p. 47.

The collection contains five immature specimens from Gready Harbor, Labrador, and from Indian Harbor, Labrador. The smallest specimens show the earliest stages in the formation of the canal system, in which they agree closely with the figures of L. Agassiz ('62).

CYANEA ARCTICA Péron and Lesueur.

Cyanea arctica PÉRON and LESUEUR, '09, p. 51.

The collection contains two young specimens of this common species from Indian Harbor, Labrador, August 12; surface.

CTENOPHORÆ.

PLEUROBRACHIA PILEUS (Fabricius).

Beroe pileus FABRICIUS, 1780, p. 361.
Pleurobrachia pileus VANHÖFFEN, '95, p. 21.

St. Pierre, Newfoundland, October 1, 6 specimens, all about 14 mm. high.

This species is common in both American and European waters, as well as in Greenland. (Chun, '98, p. 15.)

MERTENSIA OVUM (Fabricius).

Beroe ovum FABRICIUS, 1780, p. 362.
Mertensia ovum MÖRCH, '57, p. 97.

This well-known boreal species is represented by three specimens from 30 miles southeast of Nain, Labrador, August 15, and two specimens from Gready Harbor, Labrador, August 8, all 8–10 mm.

in height. The voracity of this form is well illustrated by the fact that one individual had entirely engulfed a young sculpin (*Acanthocottus grœnlandicus* Fabricius) no less than 21 mm. long, the victim being doubled up so as to fit into the digestive cavity of its captor.

M. ovum is a common species in the cold waters north of Cape Cod, whither it is swept by the Labrador current, but it is of only sporadic occurrence south of that dividing line. So far as known the Woods Hole region marks the extreme limit of its southward dispersal in American waters. It is known both from Greenland and from Spitzbergen, and is probably of circumpolar occurrence (Chun, '98, p. 10).

BEROE CUCUMIS Fabricius.

Beroe cucumis FABRICIUS, 1780, p. 361.

Between Cape Sable and Cape Race, July 19, about 100 small specimens, 3–14 mm. high; St. Pierre, off Newfoundland, October 1, 1 specimen, 15 mm. high; Fogo Island, Newfoundland, July 29, 5 specimens, 40–50 mm. high.

Unfortunately the large specimens were all so fragmentary that it was impossible to trace the course of the stomachic canals with any accuracy. However, since these appear to end blindly, the specimens must be referred to *B. cucumis* rather than to *B. ovata*. In the small specimens the blind terminations of the canals were easily traced. *B. cucumis* was taken on the Plankton Expedition in the Labrador current (Chun, '98, p. 27), and is known to be widely distributed throughout Arctic regions. On the coast of the United States it is known to occur as far south as Cape Cod, whither it is no doubt carried by the Labrador current.

BIBLIOGRAPHY.

AGASSIZ, A., '62a. On the Mode of Development of the Marginal Tentacles of the Free Medusæ of some Hydroids. Proc. Boston Soc. Nat. Hist., vol. 9, pp. 88–103, 31 figs.
——— '62b. In Agassiz, L., '62.
——— '65. North American Acalephæ. Mem. Mus. Comp. Zoöl., Harvard Coll., vol. 1, xiv + 334 pp., 360 figs.
AGASSIZ, L., '49. Contributions to the Natural History of the Acalephæ of North America. Pt. 1. On the Naked-eyed Medusæ, etc. Mem. Am. Acad. (N. S.), vol. 4, pp. 221–316, 8 pls.
——— '62. Contributions to the Natural History of the United States of America, Vol. 4, Monogr. 2, viii + 372 + (12) pp., pls. 20–35.
ALLMAN, G. J., '64. On the construction and limitation of genera among the Hydroida. Ann. Mag. Nat. Hist., ser. 3, vol. 13, pp. 345–380.
——— '78. Hydrozoa, in Capt. Sir G. S. Nares' Narrative of a Voyage to the Polar Sea during 1875–76, in H. M. Ships "Alert" and "Discovery." London, 1878, vol. 2, pp. 290–292, 3 figs.
BIGELOW, H. B., :09. Reports on the Scientific Results of the Expedition to Eastern Tropical Pacific, etc. XVI. The Medusæ. Mem. Mus. Comp. Zool., Harvard Coll., vol. 37, 243 pp., 48 pls.
BÖHM, R., '78. Helgolander Leptomedusen. Jena. Zeit. f. Naturw., vol. 12, pp. 68–203, pls. 2–7.
BRANDT, J. F., '38. Ausführliche Beschreibung der von C. H. Mertens auf seiner Weltumsegelung beobachteten Schirmquallen. . . . Mém. Acad. St. Pétersbourg, vol. 4, pt. 2, pp. 237–411, pls. 1–31.
BROCH, H., :05. Zur Medusenfauna von Norwegen. Bergens Mus. Aarbog, 1905, no. 11, 8 pp.
BROWNE, E. T., '95. Report on the Medusæ of the L. M. B. C. District. Trans. Liverpool Biol. Soc., vol. 9, pp. 243–286.
——— '96. On British Hydroids and Medusæ. Proc. Zool. Soc. London, 1896, pp. 459–500, pls. 16, 17.
——— '97. On British Medusæ. Proc. Zool. Soc. London, 1897, pp. 816–835, pls. 48, 49.
——— :03. Report on some Medusæ from Norway and Spitzbergen. Bergens Mus. Aarbog, 1903, no. 4, 36 pp., 5 pl.
CHUN, C., '88. Die Siphonophoren der kanarischen Inseln. Sitzungsber. Akad. Wiss. Berlin, vol. 44, pp. 1141–1173.
——— '98. Die Ctenophoren der Plankton Expedition. . . . Ergebnisse der Plankton Exped. . . . vol. 2, K. a., 32 pp., 3 pls.
CLARK, H. JAMES, '63. Prodromus of the History, Structure and Physiology of the Order Lucernariæ. Journ. Boston Soc. Nat. Hist., vol. 7, pp. 531–567.
ESCHSCHOLTZ, FR., '29. System der Acalephen, eine ausführliche Beschreibung aller medusenartigen Strahlthiere. vi + 190 pp., 16 pls. Berlin, F. Dummler, 1829.
FABRICIUS, O., 1780. Fauna grœnlandica. Hafniæ et Lipsiæ, xvi + 452 pp., 1 pl., 1780.
FEWKES, J. W., '81. Studies of the Jelly-Fishes of Narragansett Bay. Bull. Mus. Comp. Zool., Harvard College, vol. 8, no. 8, pp. 141–182, 10 pls.
FORBES, E., '48. A Monograph of British Naked-eyed Medusæ. 104 pp., 13 pls., Ray Soc., London, 1848.
FORSKÅL, P., 1775. Descriptiones animalium . . . quæ in itinere orientale observavit. Hauniæ, edidit Carstem Niebuhr, 1775, 20, xxxiv + 164 pp.
——— 1776. Icones rerum naturalium quas in itinere orientali depingi curavit Petrus Forskål . . . edidit Carstem Niebuhr. Hauniæ, 1776, 15 pp., 43 pls.

GRÖNBERG, G., '98. Die Hydroidmedusen des Arktischen Gebietes. Zool. Jahrb., Syst. Abt., vol. 11, pp. 451–467, pl. 27.

HAECKEL, E., '79. Das System der Medusen. Part 1: System der Craspedoten. Jena. Denkschr., vol. 1, xxv + 360 pp., atlas of 40 pls.

——— '81. Report on the Deep Sea Medusæ . . . Report on the scientific results of the voyage of H. M. S. "Challenger." Zoology, vol. 4, no. 2, cv + 154 pp., 32 pls.

HARGITT, C. W., :05. The Medusæ of the Woods Hole Region. Bull. U. S. Bureau of Fisheries, vol. 24, pp. 21–79, pls. 1–7.

HARTLAUB, C., '97. Hydromedusen Helgolands. Zweiter Ber. Wissensch. Meeresunters., (new ser.), vol. 2, pp. 49–516, pls. 14–23, Kiel und Leipzig, 1897.

——— :07. Craspedote Medusen. 1. Theil, 1 Lief.: Codoniden und Cladonemiden. In Nordisches Plankton, 12, Kiel, etc., 1907, 135 pp., 1 pl.

LINNÉ, K. VON, 1766–1768. Systema Naturæ, etc. 12 ed. Holmiæ, 1766–1768.

MAAS, O., '97. Die Medusen. Reports on an Exploration off the West Coasts of Mexico, etc. Mem. Mus. Comp. Zoöl., Harvard Coll., vol. 23, no. 1, 92 pp., 15 pls.

——— :04. Méduses provenant des Campagnes des yachts "Hirondelle" et "Princesse-Alice" (1886–1903). Résultats des Camp. Sci., etc., par Albert 1er, Prince Souverain de Monaco, fasc. xxviii, 71 pp., 6 pls.

——— :05. Die Craspedoten Medusen der Siboga-Expedition. Uitkom. op. Zool. Bot., Oceanogr. en Geol. Gebied. Siboga-Expeditie. Monogr. x, 84 pp., 14 pls.

——— :06. Die Arktischen Medusen. Fauna Arctica. Vol. 4, pp. 480–526.

MÖRCH, O., '57. Nat. Bid. til en Beskr. af Grönland, 1857.

NUTTING, C. C., '99. The Hydroids of the Woods Hole Region. Bull. U. S. Bureau of Fisheries, vol. 19, pp. 325–386, 105 figs.

PÉRON, F., and LESUEUR, C. A., '09. Histoire Générale et Particulière de tous les Animaux qui composent la Famille des Méduses. Ann. Mus. Hist. Nat., vol. 14, pp. 218–228.

SARS, M., '35. Beskrivelser og Jagttagelser, etc., Bergen, 1835, xii+82 pp., 15 pls.

VANHÖFFEN, E., '89. Versuch einer Natürlichen Gruppierung der Anthomedusen. Zool. Anz., vol. 14, pp. 439–446.

——— '95. Die Grönlandischen Ctenophoren (Zool. Ergeb. der Grönland-Exped., vol. 2). Bibl. Zool., pt. 20, pp. 15–21.

——— '97. Die Fauna und Flora Grönlands. "In Drygalski's Grönland-Expedition der Gesell. für Erdkunde zu Berlin, 1891–1893, vol. 2, pt. 1, 10+383 pp." [Medusæ, pp. 272–274, pl. 2.]

——— :02. Die Craspedoten Medusen der Deutschen Tiefsee-Expedition, 1898–1899. I. Trachymedusen. Wiss. Ergeb. Deutsch. Tiefsee-Expedition, vol. 3, pp. 53–88, pls. 9–12.

——— :08. Die Narcomedusen. Wiss. Ergeb. Deutsch. Tiefsee-Expedition, vol. 19, pp. 43–73, pls. 7–9.

EXPLANATION OF PLATES.

(All figures are from photographs of preserved specimens.)

PLATE 30.

Fig. 1. *Sarsia princeps*, specimen 14 mm. high. The jagged outlines of the radial canals are visible. *c. ap.*, apical canal.
2. *Sarsia mirabilis*, specimen 10 mm. high. *o*, ocellus.
3. *Catablema vesicaria*. A mature specimen 17 mm. in diameter. The bell is opened and its walls turned aside to show the manubrium and the vertical sexual folds (*go.*) in the interradii. *c. ra.*, radial canal; *L*, lip.
4. *Catablema vesicaria*, young specimen 9 mm. in diameter. The radial canals (*c. ra.*) already bear glandular diverticula, but the margin of the circular canal (*c. c.*) is still smooth.
5. *Tiara pileata*. Segment of bell-wall and margin. The radial canal (*c. ra.*) shows lateral diverticula, but the circular canal (*c. c.*) is smooth.

PLATE 31.

Fig. 1. *Melicertum campanula*. One octant of bell margin of specimen 12 mm. in diameter showing fully developed tentacles (T^1), small tentacles (T^2), and rudimentary tentacles in the form of cirri (*ci*). *go*, gonad.
2. *Bougainvillea superciliaris*. Side view of specimen 5.5 mm. in diameter.
3. *Lizzia octopunctata*. Side view of a budding individual 3.5 mm. in diameter.
4. Oral view of another individual of the same size. *T. Ra.*, radial, *T. ira.*, interradial tentacle-group.
5. *Lizzia octopunctata*. Lip (*L*) showing nematocyst knobs (*nem.*).
6. *Catablema vesicaria*. Segment of bell showing glandular diverticula on both radial canal (*c. ra.*) and circular canal (*c. c.*), and the form of the basal tentacular bulbs, especially in the case of the radial tentacle (*T. Ra.*), which is turned to one side. *g*, gelatinous substance of bell.
7. *Tiara pileata*. Dissection of margin of bell to show lateral aspect of tentacular bulb. *c. c.*, lumen of circular canal. *g*, gelatinous substance of bell.

PLATE 32.

Fig. 1. *Melicertum campanula*. One octant of margin of medium-sized individual 6 mm. in diameter showing tentacles in various stages of development. *go.*, gonad.
2. *Æginopsis laurentii*. Side view of specimen 7 mm. in diameter, showing the conformation of the gastric pockets (*g. p.*) and their separation in the radii of the peroniæ (*Per.*). *T*, tentacle.
3. Aboral view of another individual of about the same size. *Per.*, peronia.
4. Oral view of gastric wall of individual 1.5 mm. in diameter. Lettering as in fig. 2, *L*, lip.
5. Oral view of gastric wall of specimen 13 mm. in diameter, to show sexual folds (*go.*). *Per.*, peronia; *g*, gelatinous substance; *L*, lip; *T*, tentacle.
6. Otocyst, with otolith (*otl.*). × 200.

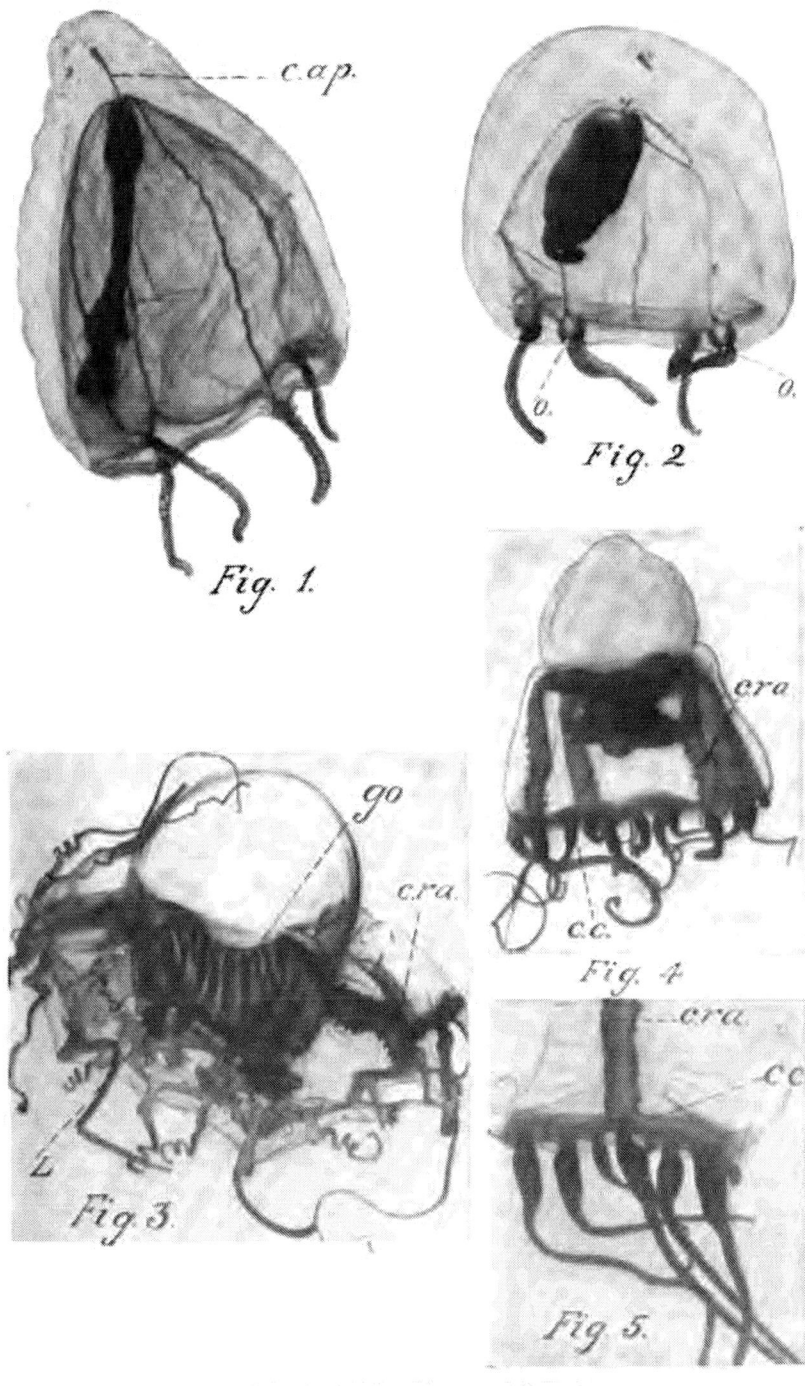

LABRADOR AND NEWFOUNDLAND MEDUSÆ.

FOR EXPLANATION OF PLATE SEE PAGE 320.

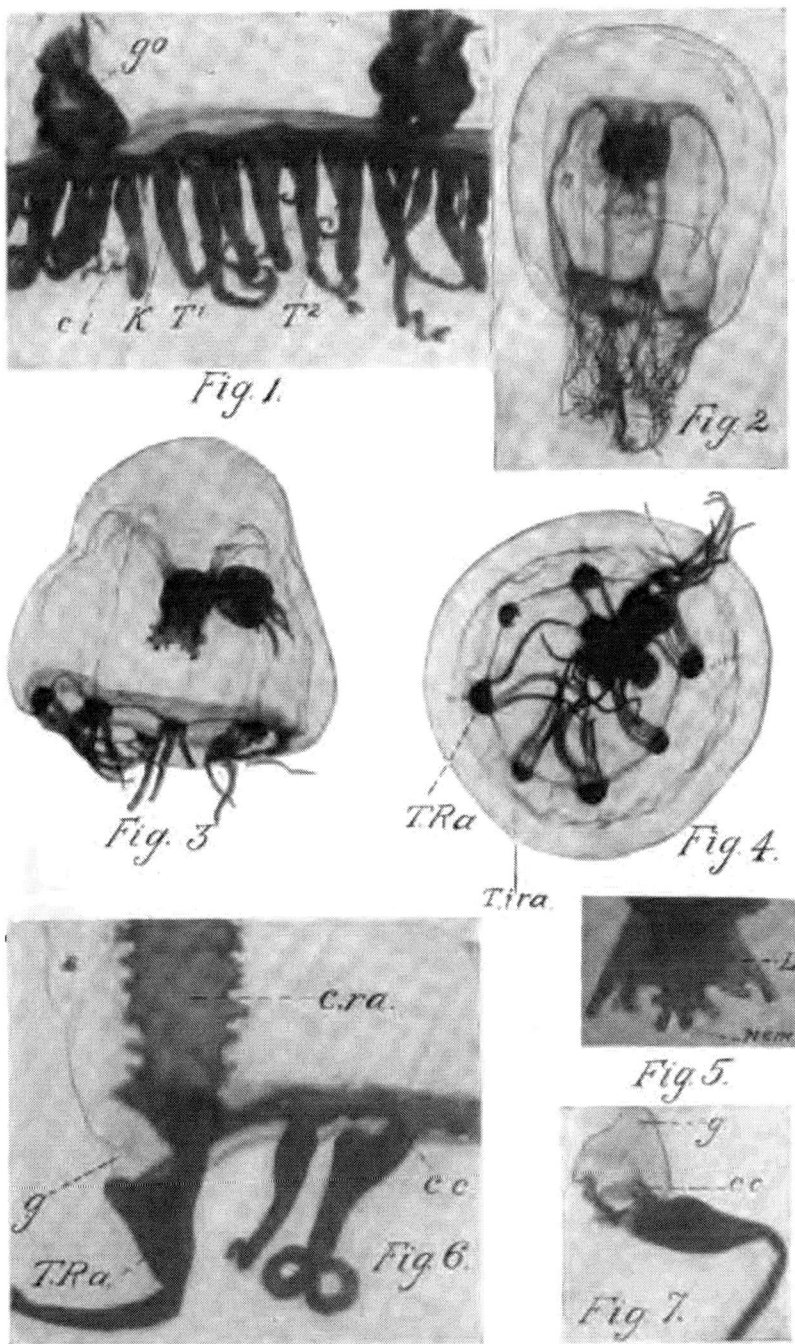

LABRADOR AND NEWFOUNDLAND MEDUSÆ.

FOR EXPLANATION OF PLATE SEE PAGE 320.

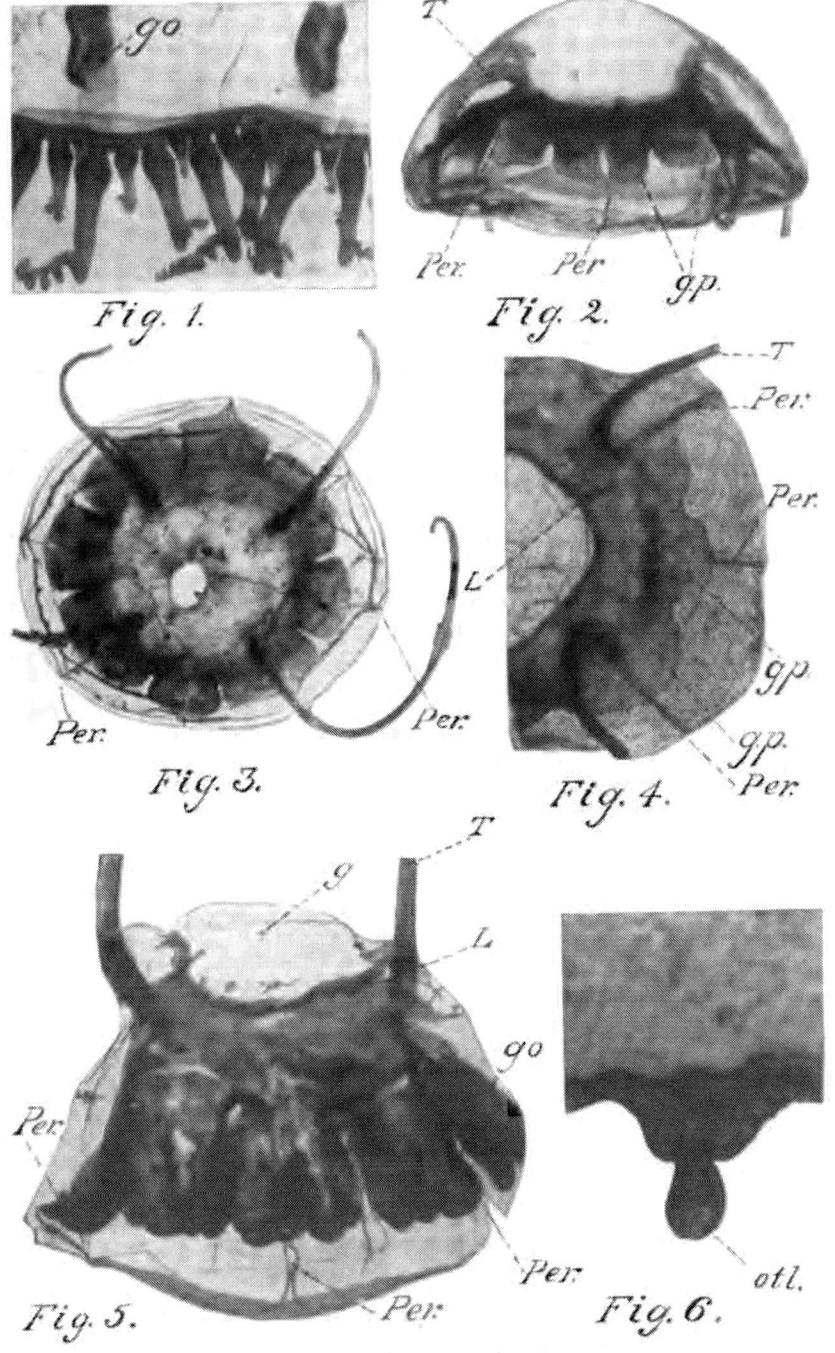

LABRADOR AND NEWFOUNDLAND MEDUSÆ.

FOR EXPLANATION OF PLATE SEE PAGE 320.

Printed by Libri Plureos GmbH in Hamburg, Germany